Serenity

Xiyun Hu

BookLeaf Publishing

India | USA | UK

Presentation by *BookLeaf Publishing*

Web: www.bookleafpub.com

E-mail: info@bookleafpub.com

ISBN: 9789357445054

First edition 2022

Your Voice

Words can't make a song
You cannot hear melodies with letters.
But your voice sounds like an orchestra
Playing the most beautiful song I've ever heard.

Clouds

Everyone loves sunny days
But what they dont see
Is what the rain clouds hold.
They're full of emotion,
Layers.
But people are distracted
By the glimmering sun
To see what the cloudy skies bring.

' A '

It's just a letter
But it matters so much.
Its just a letter
That I'll never get.
Its just a letter
That shows others who I am.
Its just a letter
But its more than I'll ever be able to do.

Laughter

Some laugh because they're relieved,
Gasps of relief on what they've achieved.
Some do it to hide their pain,
Pain that's too hard to explain.
Some laugh to hide their fear.
Hoping that it's not near.
But maybe one day
Everything will be okay,
There will no longer be a decoy,
And the world will be filled with laughs of joy.

Dreaming

Its the same word.
Spelled the same,
Spoken the same,
And maybe, they do mean the same.
I guess it can mean different things,
But words don't sprout angel wings.
Although, your dreams when you sleep aren't real.
The dreams that are hopes for what we obtain,
Doesn't seem possible to attain.

Empty

I thought I'd never feel this again,
Didn't even wonder when.
I guess I was right,
Never thought I'd reach this height.
With this height now I fall,
I feel nothing at all.

Finir

I hate finishing notebooks.
When those pages get filled with writing,
It means that the story has ended.
There are no more plot twists,
New characters,
Or even beautiful metaphors.
The only thing left,
Is a story, that nobody will read.

Dissolve

Sometimes, the moon and stars
Is all I have.
But as my vision blur further,
They too,
Start fading away.

Flame

As they snuff out your flame,
There's nothing you can do
But to watch.
They say that you're the blame,
One of the only few
That burned till you're botched.
As the last bit of smoke
Trail out into the wind,
Smell its essence one last time.
One day, your flame will burn prime.

Nails

I pick at my nails.
They aren't perfect,
They get in the way.
When I get nervous,
They would be the first I attack.
When I see other people's nails,
They all look beautiful.
With acrylics they shine,
And polishes creating patterns.
But my nails are never pretty
They just get in the way.
I am my nails.

Ne

Only under a certain type of light.
The black light,
Can neon colors truly shine.
I wonder,
If I'll ever find my purple rays
To be able to show the world how much I can
glow.

Fights

I've always seen it as physical,
Everyone's being critical.
People pushing and shoving,
The others are running.
Screams fill the room,
All with a sense of doom.
For whatever they've done,
Even if there is none.
But in reality,
A flaw of our mortality,
The fights everyday
In every way,
The uncontrolled spread,
Are the ones inside our head.

Deadline

In a world that's filled with deadlines,
Only a few make the headlines.
We live in a deadline.
It's just a matter,
A simple chatter
Of when our deadline is.

Flicker

It's the small moments that you treasure.
Like the look of a skyline,
Or the colors of a sunset.
Maybe it's winning,
Or even losing.
But it doesn't matter.
It's the experience.
That's what makes life memorable.

Kairosclerosis

I finally stopped.
I stopped to listen,
But not to my thoughts this time.
I ignored the memories from the past,
And worries about the future.
I stopped,
And I felt what it's like to live.

60 Seconds

60 seconds.
It seems a lot more than 1 minute.
But when you stop focusing
And let time fly,
60 seconds is all it takes
For everything to change.

The End

"Everything must come to an end,"
That's true.
Reality is often worse than pretend.
Not when it comes to you,
There's no way to end it
Until the final bit.
When the sun turns the skies red,
And the trees gold.
There wont be another day for you to dread.
The end may not be said.

Peak

The hardest part of the climb
Is the part where you're about to give up.
Glancing at the clock but not knowing the time,
Pouring water but not filling the cup.
Catch yourself when you're about to plummet,
You're about to reach the summit.

Chance

Take it or you lose it.
Sometimes its too hard to admit,
Just how hard trying can be.
Everything is worth to some degree,
But nothing is worth it, if there's no risk.
You hope to make it go away in a whisk,
But nothing, after all, has no costs.

Despair

There will always be someone better,
Someone who will shine brighter than the sun.
To me, they're exactly what someone is.
Billions of others that will never forget her
Vibrant light that sparkled because she won.
Never will she fail a quiz,
She writes perfection with every letter.
When she speaks, they will never run,
Nobody's voice is as angelic as this.

Serenity

Nothing can be fixed with an apology.
Even with that knowledge he
Still wouldn't get the stars for me.
After knowing where I would be,
He will never see my scars ignite.
If only I can take flight,
Into space where the stars reside.
Maybe then, I can get the star you failed to
provide.

www.ingramcontent.com/pod-product-compliance
Lightning Source LLC
LaVergne TN
LVHW051252200726
843510LV00011B/1811